Dedicated to my daughter, Carly Hope!

To my Daughter:
You inspire me to be a better person every day. Your compassion and loving kindness towards everyone you meet fills me with joy. I strive to be more like you. Thank you for supporting and encouraging me to write this book.

I love you beautifuls!

You Can Sit With Us!

Author: Tisha Whittington

Illustrator: Leigha Briolo

In a school down the road from yours, there were different groups of animals who loved to hang out during lunchtime.

There were the popular peacocks, always showing off their colorful feathers and checking their phones for new followers.

Nearby, the trendy turtles were busy
learning and filming the latest TikTok
dance, their moves perfectly matching and
capturing the attention of all watching.

At another table, the fabulous flamingos were having fun making fancy friendship bracelets and taking photos together, capturing happy moments with big smiles.

Meanwhile, the cute crawfish were painting their tiny claws with bright colors and braiding colorful strands of hair, giggling and chatting about their day.

At another table were lively groups of athletes, including bouncing bears, energetic elephants, and playful pelicans. They hurried through their lunch, eager to rush outside to play sports with their friends.

In the middle of all this excitement, a shy gator named, "Nola, arrived at school.
Nola didn't know anyone and felt a bit nervous about finding friends to sit with at lunch.

She watched the different groups, hoping to find a place where she could join in and feel welcomed. Nola tried to approach each table, but she was met with excuses or giggles that made her feel left out.

The peacocks and turtles were focused on their phone screens and dances; they didn't even see Nola.

Meanwhile, the flamingos and crawfish were too busy with their creative activities.

The athletes at another table were wild
with energy, talking excitedly about plans
for the afternoon games.

Feeling a bit left out and sad, Nola sat alone in a quiet corner, nibbling on her lunch and wondering if she would ever find friends to sit with.

Just then, a friendly bunny named Bella noticed Nola sitting by herself. "Hey there! Would you like to sit with us? Bella asked with a warm smile.

Nola's eyes lit up with happiness. She nodded eagerly, and Bella led her to a table where a mix of animals---rabbits, alligators, birds, and deer--- were enjoying their lunch and chatting happily.

Nola felt welcomed and included as she joined Bella and her new friends. They talked about their favorite things, told jokes, and shared their candy with each other. Nola realized that she had found a place where she could be herself and have fun with others.

As the days went by, Nola continued to sit with Bella and their group, and she also started to chat with other animals from different tables. Slowly, the school became a friendlier place where everyone felt accepted and happy to sit together, sharing stories and laughter.

No one felt left out or lonely anymore because everyone knew that in this school, "You Can Sit With Us," was the rule that mattered- a rule of kindness, inclusion, and acceptance in both the digital and real worlds, on the playing field, at the art corner, and in the cafeteria!